Schools Then

by Cynthia Swain

I need to know these words.

bench

desk

notebook

tablet

The girl has a log school.

The girl has a brick school.

The boy has a **bench**.

The boy has a **desk**.

The girl has a **tablet**.

The girl has a **notebook**.

The girl has a computer!